The Bigger Picture:

The second poetic collection

by

Esperanza Habla

© 2016 La Luna Press

Previously copyrighted as:
Just Me: The Creative Collective Poetic Works of Esperanza Habla Volume 2

ISBN: 978-0-9915104-3-6

Library of Congress Control Number: 2016932624

Cover design and all photographs by Esperanza Habla
Author portrait courtesy of Kristen Pugh Photography
Logo for La Luna Press by Adam Whitaker

All rights reserved. No part of this publication may be reproduced, distributed, or transmitted in any form or by any means, including photocopying, recording, or other electronic or mechanical methods, without the prior written permission of the publisher, except in the case of brief quotations embodied in critical reviews and certain other noncommercial uses permitted by copyright law.

For permission requests, write to the publisher, at the address below.

La Luna Press, L.L.C.
P.O. Box 533284
Indianapolis, IN
46253
USA

Thank you for purchasing this book.

For more information, please visit us at:

www.lalunapress.com

Thank you to my dear family for their never-ending love and support:

Amy, David, Debbie, Diane, Hope, John, Johnny, Kristi, Marjorie, Megan, Wayne

Thank you also to my dear friends:

A, A, B, R, M, X, P, C, L

Finally, to my dear friend Sally.

Rest in peace my dear friend.

See you in the moon.

Table of Contents:

The Bigger Picture……………………….	1
Unconditional………………………….	3
The Cat With the Heart on Her Back…..	4
Just Me…………………………………	5
One More Star in the Sky……………..	6
Poetess…………………………………	7
Warm Blanket…………………………	8
The Reason……………………………	9
Promises………………………………	12
The Candle……………………………	13
I Need to Fly…………………………..	14
Love Again……………………………	15
Letter to the Moon…………………….	16
The Book………………………………	17
Waiting…………………………………	18
Nothing to Fix…………………………	19
The Words of a Poet…………………..	21
Games…………………………………	23
My Eternal Best Friend………………..	24
Addicted………………………………	25
Artist…………………………………..	28
High Point……………………………..	29
Snow……………………………………	31
KnoW More……………………………	32
A Thank You…………………………..	33
Welcome………………………………	34
Letters to the Moon……………………	35
My Voice………………………………	36
Where were You?.................................	38
Enough is Enough……………………..	40
'Tis the Season…………………………	42
Judgment………………………………	43
Writing a Book………………………..	44
Lessons from 2012…………………….	45
My Story………………………………	48
Indigo Colored Glasses……………….	51
Meetings and Partings…………………	52
Old Friends……………………………	53

Gratitude…………………………………	54
Living History……………………………	55
Ode to Inspiration……………………...	56
Acts of Kindness…………………………	57
Forgiveness………………………………	59
The Gift of the Moon……………………..	61
Dedication………………………………..	62
The Smiling Moon………………………..	64
Trust………………………………………	65
The Adventures of Kit and Caboodle….	67
Building a Legacy………………………..	69
A Life of Words…………………………	71
The Journey………………………………	72
Poetry……………………………………..	74
Loss………………………………………	75
Infinite Possibilities…………………….	78
My Dear Sally……………………………	79
Respect…………………………………..	83
The Moon…………………………………	84
Creating a Destiny………………………..	86
The Writer's Eye………………………..	88
Blissfully Foolish………………………..	89
Citizen of the World…………………...	90
Confidence………………………………..	93

The Bigger Picture   June 22, 2012

I recently wrote about the death of a friendship. We were very good friends to one another. But the last days of the friendship were very painful. This person was a genuine friend to me. We loved one another as friends. We shared many wonderful moments, had many fascinating discussions, had many moments of laughter and shared our deepest hurts, fears and darkest secrets.

Whenever one of us had a problem, or just needed to talk, we were always there for one another-to listen, give advice, provide comfort, support, make each other laugh. The sudden transition of this person not being in my life anymore, after our years of friendship, is a definite change. There are two sides to every story. On one hand, there is that person's view of things, and on the other hand is reality.

Do I wish that person would have handled things differently? Yes. Do I wish I had a chance to explain my reaction to the last issue in our friendship, to convey that what I felt had nothing to do with that person? Yes. But none of that matters. It's in the past. It's done. What truly matters is what happens now. I went to a good friend of mine, a wise author I know (and mutual friend of that person and myself) and told him what has happened. He was very sorry to hear what had happened. But, he also gave me the best advice.

My author friend pointed out that I could keep thinking about the end of the friendship, and how hurtful and disrespectful it was. Or, I could look at the bigger picture. I can look back on the friendship as it was over the years. I can look at the good times we shared, the great discussions we had together, the times we made each other laugh, everything that I learned, the time when our friendship was sweet and good. He also said

The Bigger Picture

that I can be thankful. I can be thankful to God for sending that person into my life. I can thank God for our years of friendship and the life lessons that the friendship taught me.

I can be thankful that that person was indeed a good friend to me and loved me for who I am, flaws and all. That is what I plan to do now. I plan to look past the hurt. I plan to be thankful that that person and I had the chance to meet.

Picture yourself at the beach at the ocean. You're sitting on a towel, enjoying the breeze, soaking in the rays of sun. There are many people with you at the beach, and many distractions-

people fighting, yelling, people smoking cigars, children screaming, cell phones ringing, loud music blaring, dogs barking-all of which is disrupting your peace.

Do you focus on those distractions? Or do you instead choose to focus on the beautiful, infinite ocean just ahead of you?

That's what I choose to look at. The ocean. The bigger picture.

"The Bigger Picture" by Esperanza Habla
Taken on Mackinac Island, 2009

The Bigger Picture

Unconditional   June 28, 2012

I've often heard the word "unconditional", used in conjunction with "love" and "forgiveness." Two words that are inherently conditional.

Unconditional love, as a concept, sounds beautiful.

100% acceptance for who and what you are.

But that acceptance doesn't equate to being unconditional.

My life, my relationships, my friendships, all are conditional.

Certain conditions have to be met for me to stay in your life.

You have to treat me decently. You have to treat me with respect.

You have to be honest with me.

You have to treat me as your equal, a person worthy of respect and love.

If these conditions are not met, cannot be met, you cannot be in my life.

Respect is given where respect is given.

Love and forgiveness are conditional.

I am conditional.

Unconditional anything doesn't exist.

The Bigger Picture

The Cat with the Heart on Her Back   July 2, 2012

(A conversation between my cat and me the other day)

You want to be brushed? You used to hate to be brushed. Okay, I'll brush you. Oh, does that feel good? Yeah? Your purring, and clawing the air, tells me "yes." You used to hate it when I did this. Now you can't get enough. Hey, I forgot about that. You have a heart on your back. A little orange heart. I totally forgot about that.

We won't have many more days together. You won't get to be brushed anymore. You know, if you have to go, if you need to go, before the day comes, you just go. I will understand. That will be a truly generous gift to me. Don't you worry about me. I'm going to be just fine. You've been a great kitty. I hope I've been a great person to you. Yeah, I'm your person. You're my kitty and I'm your person. Is that enough brushing?

Okay, you're walking away. You're done. Goodbye my dear friend.

"The Heart" by Esperanza Habla

The Bigger Picture

Just Me   July 4, 2012

What do you read when you read a poem? A thought?
An emotion? A collection of words? My heart? My soul?

What is a poem? A snapshot in time? A time capsule of
thoughts and emotions? A window into the writer's soul?

I think, when you read one of my poems, you're reading me.

Just me.

"Self Portrait" by Esperanza Habla

The Bigger Picture

One More Star in the Sky   July 7, 2012

I have known this day was coming. I had been given signs to look for. Some of them had appeared. Most didn't. The death of a pet can be a painful event. To some people, a pet is a cherished family member, or even a child. To me, I feel like I have lost a friend. Yesterday, I lost my cat, Calypso. She was my constant companion for 17 years. A truly great friend. She had lost most of her hearing, and had many issues with mobility. She was in pain, and her quality of life had begun to diminish. The time had come. It was the bravest, most selfless thing I have ever done. This wasn't for me. It was for her. I had never experienced anything like that before. I was anxious leading up to the event, not knowing what to expect. But I knew within my soul that I was making the right decision. Her passing was so serene and peaceful. She literally went to sleep. The veterinarian was very caring and compassionate. She walked me through every step, explaining everything, which put me at ease. There was no tremor, no last gasps, no screeching. Just sleep. Just peace. I played music during the event. I chose music from the group Celtic Woman. The first song below, "Caledonia", was a special song to her. I sang her the chorus. The second song, "The Parting Glass," a song of farewell, was playing as she died. My friend has gone. There is now one more star in the sky. She had a long life, and she is at peace. And so am I.

Good night my pretty girl.

"Calypso the Cat,"
by Esperanza Habla

The Bigger Picture

Poetess   July 13, 2012

I am a poet; I create poems with my palette of words. I am a translator; I help authors reach audiences in other languages. I am a singer; I fill a room with my voice. I am an author; I can write a story to move the sternest heart. I am not an actor or director or clown or mime. I am not a model, not a statue. I am a writer. I live a life in the arts. I may not have your opinions, your views. I may not have your talents, your gifts. But your talents are just as special as mine. Your skills, what you bring to the world, are just as valid as mine. You have changed the world with your art. And so have I.

What am I? I am a writer, a translator, a singer, a poet. A citizen of the world. A person living a life in the arts. Does that make me an artist? Maybe. A person that contributes to society? I hope so.

I hope my words have meaning. I hope my words can help someone who is going through the same situation. I hope my words brighten someone's day.

I don't care if my skills, my talents are different than yours. I respect them all the same. I am a fellow creator in the arts. I will celebrate your talents and skills as I hope you will celebrate mine.

As creators, artists, we all deserve respect. We are part of a rich community that demands it. I am proud to be in this community. A community where each creator's talents are appreciated and celebrated.

I belong in this community. I am of this community.

Because I am a poet.

The Bigger Picture

Warm Blanket   July 21, 2012

Support is such an important thing.

From friends, family, co-workers, social networking friends.

Such an important thing.

Reaching out to someone, letting them know you are thinking about them, means so much.

I have been on the receiving end of much support recently.

It has been very comforting to receive such love and support.

I have felt very protected, cared about and loved.

The love and support I have experienced has been like a warm blanket, protecting me, comforting me, providing me solace in my time of need.

I know I am loved. I know I am not alone.

Many thanks to my family and my friends:

A, L, M, R, A, L, G, J, E, B, H, E

Thank you for your love and support.

It means more to me than you will ever know.

The Reason

August 8, 2012

I love social networking. It allows me to meet and get to know my readers, as well as artists from all around the world. People I would normally never have the chance to meet. It is also a tool for self-promotion, as well as promoting projects of others as well. It is also a wonderful way to make friends.

This past week I had conversations with two friends, on the same day in fact. They both were upset, and I sent them a message through a social networking site to talk about what was bothering them. These two people had the same problem, or same occurrence happening in their lives at the same time- they had a broken heart. These friends are new in my online social circle, so I didn't know exactly what they needed-either someone to listen to what they had to say, or just someone to send a supportive word or positive thought their way.

I did what I knew to do-I asked them what was wrong and listened as they told me what was wrong. They needed someone to listen to them and to be heard. I listened to them and heard them, and expressed my regret about what happened, and what they were going through.

I then had a thought. I have recently gone through something similar, so I thought reading about my experience might help them. I sent them the poem "The Bigger Picture." Both of these gentlemen read the poem, and then wrote me back.

They thanked me for sending them the poem. They were stuck in the hurt and hadn't thought to look at it from a different perspective. They were so appreciative and thankful to read the poem. They knew someone else felt what they felt, and that they weren't alone. And, more importantly, they didn't have to be stuck in the hurt. They could be thankful for the good times they had, and they could learn to heal and move on.

The Bigger Picture

When I began this blog, it was by invitation only. I was insecure of my talents as a poet, and I was nervous about sharing my work. I did share the blog with my closest friends, including my wise author friend. He said that I am talented as a writer and encouraged me to make the blog public. I was very insecure, and wasn't sure if I wanted to do that.

This wise author friend then pointed out all of the positives that would come with making the blog public. It would open new doors. It would allow me to meet new people and make connections all around the world, and be a platform for my writings and future literary endeavors. Those were all nice things to say, but I still wasn't convinced. Then he said the phrase that changed my mind-

"Maybe someone will read something you've written and it will help them with something they're going through. Maybe you can be of help to someone."

That was the reason. The reason I made this blog public.
I began this blog about a year and a half ago. I write poetry as inspiration strikes and publish it-I hardly ever receive any feedback about what I've written. I never know if what I have written has helped anyone, or made an impact. Until last week.

Sending these two new friends that poem did more to help them than my listening did. They read my words, and it genuinely helped them. It changed their mood, their perspective, their mindset. That was the first time that I had confirmation that anything I've written has had an impact on someone. It didn't just impact someone-two separate people-on the same day, with the same problem.

That makes it all worthwhile. The fact that my words changed how they felt, had an impact on them, that was such a powerful feeling.

I felt validated, grateful and humble at the same time.

I was moved beyond words.

To the gentleman that I helped that day, I want to tell you that you've helped me too.

Thank you so much for your thoughts and comments about what I wrote.

I am glad that I was able to make you feel better.

I'm glad that I was able to make a difference.

You've given me an amazing gift. Thank you.

That's why I made this blog public.

Because of what my friend said.

That I could help someone who was going through a similar circumstance.

It actually happened.

That's the reason.

The Bigger Picture

Promises   August 11, 2012

Promises are a tricky thing. I don't believe in promises. Well, let me go back.

I don't believe in promises that aren't kept.

It is so easy to say "I promise" to someone, in any situation.

> **"I promise to take the garbage out."**
> **"I promise I will call you tonight."**
> **"I promise I will never hurt you."**
> **"I promise I will love you forever."**

They say "rules are made to be broken"-that seems to work for promises too. I don't like promises. To me, all promises are empty. They don't mean a thing to the person who makes them easily, or asks them of you.

Promises are "pie crust promises"-easily made, easily broken. It is all too easy to break a promise. After a promise is broken, there's no going back.

I will never ask you for a promise.

Don't make me a promise if you can't keep it.

If you ask me to promise you something, specifically in the form of a promise, if I give you my promise, you can guarantee I will keep it and I will never let you down.

So if you give me your promise about something, don't break it. I in turn will keep mine.

That is if I've been foolish enough to give you my promise.

The Bigger Picture

The Candle August 11, 2012

The last three months have not been easy for me. My cat of seventeen years died. I walked away from my best friend. Those were dark, dark days. But, in the midst of the dark times, the dark days, I knew that there was a light in the darkness.

It was a candle, lit to help me through the hard times, lit by the caring and compassion and love of my friends and family to get me through the dark days. Because I had that candle, could see its flame, could feel its warmth, I knew I was not alone.

There is always a candle lit. For each one of us.

Sometimes you have to strain your eyes to see its light.

But it's there, for you.

Call it what you will: hope, spirit, faith, inspiration, belief, fortitude, comfort, awareness, help, support, caring, love, the promise of a new day.

No matter what dark times we are going through, each one of us has a candle. The light from all of our candles illuminate the world.

Whether you lit it yourself or not, the important thing is to acknowledge the candle, feel the warmth it gives out, and be enriched by the light.

> *"Look at how a single candle can both defy and define the darkness."*
> *-Anne Frank*

I Need to Fly   August 15, 2012

I have carried this a long time, this hurt, this pain. I have been able to look past the hurt, past the betrayal, past the humiliation, past being hurt on purpose. I have carried it with me, like a suitcase in hand.

At first I could not lift the suitcase. Over time things have fallen out of the suitcase, and my burden has become lighter and lighter. As I have carried this suitcase of hurt I have learned to be grateful for the times we had, the laughter we shared, the dreams we shared, the conversations we had, the stories we told, the tears we shed.

The effect on my life was absolutely amazing. I don't recognize the person I was. I am now able to live as my own person, who I really am, without hesitation.

The doors of the world opened up for me. My literary career has had a global reach, which is something I never expected. I am truly grateful for the path that I have been shown, the path I now tread.

But in the last few months of my journey, I have carried this suitcase, this weight. Hurt, betrayal, humiliation. I have reached a resting point on my journey. I am tired.

I cannot give you any of my energy anymore. I cannot carry this weight anymore. This suitcase is weighing me down. I cannot let this weigh me down anymore. I cannot stay on the ground. I need to fly.

Thank you to my friends and family for your love and support.

Thank you God for giving me the strength to leave.

The Bigger Picture

Love Again   August 23, 2012

I have found love again.

I didn't know when or where it would happen.

But, like all love, it came to me when the time was right.

I have found love in the faces of two little kittens.

They fill my home with light and love.

And I feel good knowing I rescued them and have given them a good home.

The time was right, the stars were aligned, I saw the sign, and I found love again.

"Kitteh Babies" by Esperanza Habla

The Bigger Picture

Letter to the Moon   August 28, 2012

Dear Moon, my Moon,

Hello. How are you? How are things in your world?

Things for me are fine. But they've been hard, Moon.

My friendship with him has died.

(Actually I think it was murdered.)

My feline companion went to heaven, and now is another star shining brightly, sharing your night sky.

Now, things are much better than before. I have two new little babies, little kittens to share my home and life. They are a delight. Next time you come around I will introduce you to them.

You and I have not had much time to talk of late. There were times, in the last few months that we didn't get the chance to talk together.

But I always knew you were there.

You came to me at night, to give me comfort, to let me know everything was going to be alright.

And everything is alright.

Thank you, my Moon.

Don't be a stranger, Miss Moon. Keep in touch.
    -your eternal best friend

The Book   September 18, 2012

I've written before about life, how it's seen as a dance, a movie, a game, a cabaret, a verb. For me, I have been thinking about life as a book. Our lives have a beginning, middle, and end.

Life is like a book. Everything that happens to you in life is a chapter. Time at school, relationships, friendships, all different chapters in the book of our life.

I think this is the perfect metaphor-that life is like a book. Every day of our lives we are given a blank page. What a magical gift, to get a fresh, clean blank page to start every day with.

We are also given the gift of being the author of our own stories.

You are the author of your story. You can write your story, the book of your life. Amazing.

> ***"Fiction gives us***
> ***a second chance that life denies us."***
> ***— Paul Theroux***

You're the author. It's your story. You have the power to write whatever you want, to tell whatever kind of story you want to tell, to be whatever kind of book you want it to be.

Today is a new day.

There is blank piece of paper in front of you, waiting to be filled with the words of your experiences, waiting to become chapters in the book of your life.

What's your book going to be?

The Bigger Picture

Waiting   September 27, 2012

I sit, alone at a table, pen and paper in hand, waiting.

Waiting for inspiration to come.

I can't sit down and write something phenomenal-or even good-whenever I want to.

I have to wait for inspiration to come.

Sometimes it comes, sometimes it doesn't.

I can't force it to happen-it either comes or it doesn't.

That being said, I find that I have words and phrases in my head constantly.

Words I meant to say, words I wanted to say, things I will say, things that I hope to talk about.

But I have to wait for inspiration to come, to put the pieces of the puzzle together, to put the words into phrases, to put phrases into poems, to make it all make sense.

Inspiration is like love-I can't go looking for it, it has to come to me.

I can't just write something, I have to wait for inspiration to come.

And so I sit, waiting to be inspired.

The Bigger Picture

Nothing to Fix   October 4, 2012

This week in the United States there has been an interesting discussion about weight. A viewer of a TV station wrote to a news anchor, Jennifer Livingston, commenting on her weight. As a woman of size, who some might consider "fat" and "obese," I cannot stay silent on this issue. I find that comments like this, from anyone, are cruel and unnecessary. I am a woman of size.

I am what some would call "fat." Maybe "obese" even. People who aren't "fat" or "obese" believe that we who are "fat" should lose weight to be "healthy" just like them. "Fat" is not a synonym for "unhealthy." I am here to tell you that it is possible to be "fat" and "healthy." (As long as we're talking about words, I find "fat" highly derogatory.) I have had my share of hurtful comments over the years regarding my weight.

But I'm not alone in this phenomenon-we all have something we got teased about, and in some cases, got bullied about-our weight, red hair, wearing glasses, the size of our nose, sexual orientation-the examples are endless.

I have also had people "help" me by giving me information about weight loss clinics, new fad diets, weight loss support groups, things to "help" me in my "battle of the bulge." (I use the word "help" in quotes like this because the people who said those things to me actually thought they were helping me. They were only causing me hurt and embarrassment.) I find it insulting when people give me information about losing weight. I'm sure they mean well, but it's hurtful.

If someone's health is in need of attention, no matter their size or shape, that's one thing. But being a "fat" or "obese" person isn't a problem that needs to be fixed. If you want to call me "fat", that's your choice. But I'm perfect just the way I am.

The Bigger Picture

I am a real woman. I have curves. I am beautiful and sexy as I am. I am worthy of love. My body isn't a problem that needs to be fixed. People are made in different body types. My body type is not less valid than yours. It's just a different body type. Just because my body is a different shape than yours, it doesn't make it better or worse. It's just different.

Perhaps a lesson in tolerance is needed, for people who make comments like those in the letter Mrs. Livingston received. Maybe I need to let similar comments that I've heard not affect me. Easier said than done.

I will not apologize for who or what I am. I am a real woman with curves. With curves. A real woman. I am beautiful, sexy and worthy of love. I am not a problem that needs to be fixed.

My body is not a problem that needs to be fixed.
I am perfect just the way I am. There is nothing to fix.

Esperanza Habla

The Bigger Picture

The Words of a Poet   October 16, 2012

When meeting someone new, it is common to ask what that person does for a living. Sometimes we'll then ask a question about that person's profession. But, rarely do we think to ask someone why. To me, the reason why someone is in their chosen profession is as interesting as what they do.

Quite often, in meeting new friends on social networks, I tell the person I meet, "Hi, my name is Esperanza and I am a poet in the United States." Then, usually, the person tells me what they do. I then begin to ask them questions about their profession.

> "Oh, what is that like?" "Where did you train?"
> "What is your favorite part about what you do?"

I find I learn so much about a person just by asking them about their job, what they do. It's a window into who that person is.

If someone were to ask me, **"Why are you a poet?"** I would say that my writing career began in high school. I wrote many poems about things going on in my world.

I continued writing through college, and began to write a novel. When I got a job in the real world I stopped writing. It was just something I did occasionally, and I had other things filling my life.

A couple of years ago, I was encouraged by two friends to write down what I was thinking and feeling. I found it was a way to express myself like I had never known before.

I could truly be myself. No criticisms, no judgments, just me.

The Bigger Picture

As I wrote I shared my writings with these two friends. They liked my work, how I conveyed what I felt and encouraged me to continue to write.

I never would have continued to write, or even have begun to write again, without that suggestion from these two friends.

Now that I have been writing for two years, I feel my writing is the best way I have to express myself.

I write whenever inspiration strikes-I don't write daily.

I have revisited the topic of my novel and have begun writing it again.

If I were to label myself, it would be "Poet." Or "Writer." Not "Author", not "Artist."

Although, I am now a member of a rich, vibrant, artistic community, which I never would have been otherwise.

I have readers in several countries all over the globe.

When I first began my blog, I thought just my friends and family would read it.

I didn't think anyone else would care about anything I have to say.

But my readers all over the globe have proven me wrong.

I want to thank those two friends for encouraging me to write, and to my readers for reading my words, the words of a poet.

The Bigger Picture

Games   October 27, 2012

Yesterday evening I spoke with an online friend in a social network. I had read their online status and knew they were upset. I don't know this person very well, but I wanted to talk to him, to see if he wanted to talk about something.

I contacted the person, and he said yes, he wanted to talk. He then told me about how a person he cared about had lied to him, played with his emotions, led him to believe something that wasn't true, and broke his heart. I use the word "play", as in the phrase "played with his emotions."

I think that's the perfect word-"play." That's what many people do-they play you, as if they are playing a game. Maybe that is what they are doing, playing a game.

Purposely lying to someone, making a person believe something when the opposite is really true, that is playing games with people.

Maybe there are two types of people in this world-those who will play games with people, and those who will have games played on them. Life is too short to play games with people. Have some respect for the other person-and yourself. Don't play games with people. If someone has played games with you, tell them goodbye and be on your way. Try to forget it, to heal yourself and move on; but always remember it so it never happens again.

Life is not a game. Although, there are players.

Playing with someone's emotions is not a game.

And if it is, that's one game I'm not going to play.

The Bigger Picture

My Eternal Best Friend   November 2, 2012

I saw the moon today.

I was driving in my car.

I was about to turn onto another road.

I stopped at the stop sign. I looked right, then left.

And then I saw the moon.

In the middle of a big blue sky, I saw the moon.

In the day. Almost full.

I was so surprised to see the moon out today.

Usually when the sun is out the moon is not.

But there was my friend, the moon, in the bright blue sky, in all of her glory.

She was there to wish me a good day, to tell me everything is going to be alright, to bring me comfort.

Just seeing her made me smile.

She is always there for me, my friend the moon.

My eternal best friend.

The Bigger Picture

Addicted   November 14, 2012

I think that we are addicted to language. Especially in America. The e-mail message, the status update, the smart phone app, the text, the tweet. I think that we, Americans, are addicted to language. Or, maybe I should say, addicted to our language.

I think that, because of this addiction, this has created, in some Americans, an arrogance. I have heard many people voice resentment about people immigrating to the U.S. and not speaking English. I have heard them say:

**"They're in MY country now,
they should talk to me in MY language."**

I think if a person leaves their country to move to a new one, with a new language, I think it would help them to learn the new language. But I don't think it's a requirement. Also, if Americans are traveling to other countries, some are arrogant to think that everyone around the world should know English. It is seen as an inconvenience to learn a few key phrases when traveling to a new country.

**"Why should I learn their language?
They should speak English."**

English is not the national language of the United States. The U.S. doesn't have a national language.

My social network site of choice is Facebook. I have many friends on Facebook from many countries around the world. Most of my friends are in countries in South America-Peru, Colombia, Guatemala, Nicaragua, Chile. I also have friends in Spain. The language that these online friends speak is Spanish.

I have been learning Spanish for over two years now; I am not fluent by any means, but I can communicate. When I talk to

The Bigger Picture

these online friends, I talk to them in Spanish. I never talk to them in English. It is important to me to talk to the person in their language. I never assume they know English, or that they would learn English to talk to me.

As it happens, one of these friends in South America spoke to me about this. He said,
> **"You never talk to me in English.
> You always talk to me in Spanish."**

I wrote him back, "I didn't know if you knew English. I was going to assume that you didn't." Interestingly enough, this friend is taking classes in English. We now talk to one another in English-to help him further practice and understand the language. If something isn't clear, I'll explain it in Spanish for him. But he wants to only speak in English now. He gets mad if I speak to him in Spanish. He wants to only talk in English. That makes me feel good, that he has come to me for help, to practice talking together, to help him learn my language.

I always try to talk to someone in their native language if I can. It's a form of respect. To look at me, you wouldn't think I knew a word of Spanish. But I talk to people in Spanish every day in my library. People appreciate it very much, that I have taken the time to learn their language. It makes them feel comfortable. They know that they can come to me in the future if they have a question or if there's something they don't understand and need some clarification on.

Recently I joined another social network site based out of France. The person that began the network wrote to me in English and asked me to join. He spoke to me in my language-he didn't assume I knew his. I have since made a few friends on this new social network site, most of whom do not speak English. One day, one of them wrote me an e-mail-in French.

The Bigger Picture

I didn't understand a word of it. I went to a web translator and put in what the person wrote me, so I could understand what they said. It was a lovely e-mail from an artist, telling me more about himself and his art. I then used the same web translator to write him back. I wrote, "I am using a web translator to talk to you. I'm sorry, I don't know French, but I can use this tool to speak with you. I hope the translator is doing a good job, not butchering your language, and that you can understand what I'm saying."

To my surprise, this new online friend wrote me back-in English. My communications with him from that moment on have been in English. I wrote him in French, his native language, using a web translator. I didn't assume he knew English-I made the effort to speak to him in his language. Now he makes the effort to speak to me in mine.

The reason I'm switching blogs in January, the reason I'm starting another blog and stopping writing on this blog, is because the new blog will have a "Translate" feature. You will be able to read my writing in your language. That is important to me, that you have the opportunity to read my work in your language. I'm not going to be arrogant and insist that you have to learn my language to read what I have to say.

"World of Welcome" by Esperanza Habla

The Bigger Picture

Artist   November 15, 2012

As a poet, I am a part of a rich, vibrant, global artistic community, filled with many different types of artists. But yet I do not define myself as an artist. I have shied away from that definition-or label-as "artist." Part of me feels that there is a stereotype associated with that word, of a manic depressive self-involved prima donna prone to fits of self-absorbed tantrums.

But there is another part of me that loves that word, "artist." Any writer, performer, painter, potter, anyone that does anything creative can be an artist.

To me, an artist is defined as someone who excels in their talents. A person at a level higher than a person still learning their craft. A true professional. A person with a generous spirit, readily giving guidance and support to others.

Personally, I do not see myself in either definition of that word. I don't see myself as an artist or call myself one. But in this rich, vibrant, global artistic community, my fellow artists *call me "artist."*

I have finally recognized what others see when they look at me-an artist. And so, preconceived notions and stereotypes aside, I am ready to embrace the label of artist in my definition.

I am ready to embrace the label and all of the challenges that this label brings.

My pen name is Esperanza Habla.

I am a poet, writer, translator, and an artist.

The Bigger Picture

High Point November 21, 2012

There comes a time in a person's career where they have had a great success, achieved a task, have had something truly awesome happen to them. We call these things high points. I had such a highpoint in my writing career.

A few months ago, I began following the Everyone Matters campaign via Facebook. Everyone Matters is a social media phenomenon to promote inclusiveness and, as founder Heathcliff Rothman writes, acts as:

> **"a collective message to judge others less, see the humanity in everyone, and emphasize that everyone has the right to be who they are."**

A month or so ago I made contact with the Everyone Matters campaign, and shared my recent poem, "Nothing To Fix." Then the most exciting thing happened. Heathcliff Rothman wrote me and asked me,

> **"How does being a poet make you feel? Why do you write poetry?"**

I wrote him back:

"Being a poet is amazing for me-it is the only way I can truly express myself. I can be who and what I am without any judgment or criticism. And I have a worldwide audience that reads my words, and that is very humbling to me. I began to write to express myself. I was surprised to learn that anyone would want to read what I have to say. If I can help someone with something they're going through, well, that's the reason I made a blog of my writing. Helping someone going through a similar struggle or challenge, that is amazing to me. What a gift."

The Bigger Picture

To my surprise, less than an hour later, the Everyone Matters campaign featured me on their Facebook page. Being mentioned on their page brought over 100 new readers to my blog in a day, which was amazing to me.

Even more amazing, my photo and statement appeared on the Everyone Matters Facebook page, but on their website as well. On the bottom of their website there is a feed to their Facebook page. For a day I was on the same website as such celebrities as Dame Judy Dench, Ellen Degeneres, Hugh Jackman, and Sir Paul McCartney. That is certainly an amazing high point.

My sincere thanks to Heathcliff Rothman and everyone at Everyone Matters for promoting my page on Facebook, and for promoting my blog, and giving me the greatest highpoint of my literary career.

www.everyonemattersday.com

"I'm a Poet" by Esperanza Habla

The Bigger Picture

Snow   November 29, 2012

One thing that I am all too familiar with is snow. In my area of the country, we get snow over three months of the year- December, January, and February. It is so beautiful to be home inside watching the snow fall outside. But not too much fun to drive through. When I was in college I met a young man from Brazil who was here to learn English for a job he would soon start. I remember him being fascinated the first time he saw snow fall. I didn't see the wonder in it. It's something we see every year here. It would probably be like me going to Australia and seeing a kangaroo for the first time. To me it would be amazing-to an Aussie it wouldn't be all that exciting. But I took the time to listen to my friend, to read the poem he wrote about seeing snow fall from the sky for the first time. I saw the wonder of the experience through his eyes. It was the most magical thing he'd ever seen.

This week I had a conversation with one of my online friends, who lives in South America. He said it was very hot where he lives; I wrote and told him it is the opposite here. He then asked me if it is snowing where I live. I told him that we won't have snow where I live for about another month. This then prompted further discussion about snow. My friend had seen snow on mountaintops, but had never seen snow fall, and didn't know what snow felt like. I explained that snow falls from the sky in the form of snowflakes. Every snowflake that falls is different. When a snowflake lands on your skin, the warmth of your skin makes the snow melt. It is a cold and wet sensation. I then pointed out that every snowflake has 6 points on it-or a multiple of 6 (12, 18, 24)-never 3 or 4 or 5. Always 6.

It is very beautiful to be inside, warm and cozy, safe inside your home with a cup of hot chocolate, a cat on your lap, watching the snow fall.

The Bigger Picture

KnoW More December 1, 2012

I have been watching a TV show here in the U.S. with Reverend Iyanla Vanzant. She is an author and life coach who has amazing insights. On her show one night, Iyanla was coaching a woman, and had the woman read a definition of abuse. Not physical abuse, mental, emotional abuse. The woman read the definition aloud. Here is part of what she read:

"Forms of emotional abuse include being disrespectful, discourteous, rude, condescending, patronizing, critical, judgmental, 'joking' insults, lying, repeatedly 'forgetting' promises and agreements, betrayal of trust, 'setting you up' and 'revising' history."

When I heard that quote, it resonated with me. It was like I was sitting in a dark room when suddenly every light was turned on in the room, in my house, in the universe. Does it resonate with you? Do you see yourself in this quote? Or do you see someone else in this quote, someone who has behaved this way with you? Without slandering anyone, I know now, from hearing this definition, that I have been abused. If you saw yourself in this quote, please get help. If you saw someone you love or know in this quote, and they have done this to you- or are doing this to you-get out of the relationship now. It will be the hardest thing you've ever had to do. It was for me, up until that point in my life.

There's another quote that comes to mind, from Oprah Winfrey: **"When you know better, you do better."**

I know better, and I am doing better. I will continue to do better. With this definition of emotional, spiritual abuse, my eyes will be open. At the first sign of abuse, I will be leaving that person's life. I can't do it anymore. I know more. No more.

The Bigger Picture

A Thank You   December 2, 2012

Dear friends,

I began this blog in March of 2011 with a thank you. I am now going to close this blog the same way. With a thank you. This is my last blog post on this blog. I have created a new blog for my poetry. It is called "Letters to the Moon." The new blog is highly interactive in that it has a Translate feature. You can come to the blog and pick your language. You can read my poetry, what I have to say, in your language. You will have a truly customizable reading experience. I will keep this blog up, for now, so you can still read the words of hope. However, all of my new poetry will be on the new blog. Once on the blog, the Translate feature is on the right side of the screen. There are more than 60 languages to choose from. Here is the address to the blog, so you can visit me there:

    www.letrasalaluna.blogspot.com

I also have a brand new website. I have been working on it for weeks, and it is finally ready. I am very excited to share it with you. Please go to the link below to visit my brand new site:

    www.esperanzahabla.com

I hope you will join me on this next step in my journey. My purpose is not to confuse or confound but to create a clean slate, and give you, the reader, an inclusive, customized reading experience. I want to say thank you to my friends and family and readers of this blog. Thank you to S and C for encouraging me to write in the first place. Thank you my dear friend Sally for watching over me from the moon. My guardian angel.

Thank you one and all for reading the Words of Hope.
Please join me on my new blog to read the Letters to the Moon.

The Bigger Picture

Welcome   December 1, 2012

Welcome to my new blog of poetry-Letters to the Moon.

I call myself "the Poet of the Moon," and the moon has a large presence in my life. So what better title for a blog?

I am still going to write poetry, and all of it will now be here on this blog.

I decided to start a new blog so that readers in other countries, other parts of the world could translate my work into their language.

There are over 60 languages to choose from.

Welcome.

Please, stay a while.

Relax.

Breathe.

Read my letters to the moon.

Enjoy.

www.letrasalaluna.blogspot.com

The Bigger Picture

Letters to the Moon   December 3, 2012

I sit at the computer and begin to write.

Not a letter, not a soliloquy. Maybe not a poem.

Maybe a letter. A letter to the moon.

I began to have a strong connection to the moon through a dear friend. He and I were friends from afar.

He told me once:
> **"If you miss me, if you need me, look to the moon. We're under the same moon. Look to the moon. I'm there waiting for you. You're not alone."**

When another dear true friend died, a friend told me that the friend that died was in the heavens, on the moon, watching over us, taking care of us, looking out for us like a guardian angel.

Now when I look at the moon, I do not see either of these friends. I see another friend, a new friend of my creation, Luna, who tells me:
> **"If you miss me, if you need me, look to the moon. We're under the same moon. Look to the moon. I'm there waiting for you. You're not alone."**

The moon has such a strong impact on my life. I feel the moon is a friend, a companion, a muse.

That is why I call myself the Poet of the Moon.

That is why I write her letters. Not poems.

Letters to the moon.

The Bigger Picture

My Voice   December 4, 2012

I am a person who loves music. It fascinates me. Ever since I was a little kid, I have loved music. I remember a time when I was three years old; it must have been Easter Sunday, because the choir was singing the "Halleluiah Chorus" from Georg Frideric Handel's "The Messiah." It was the most beautiful music I had ever heard.

I knew then that I wanted to be a singer. I began to sing at three years of age. I sang all through my college years, in both church and school. However, I had a setback in my teens.

I had my tonsils taken out when I was 16. The recovery from the surgery was extremely painful. (My tonsils were swollen and there was a lot of scar tissue.) It took me months to recover.

Even then, I never got my range back, and had to relearn to sing. It just wasn't the same.

Years later I went to see a specialist about my throat. The doctor explained that when my tonsils were taken out, the remaining tissue scarred during the healing process. The doctor glibly said to me:

"We can't fix it unless we take your head off."

I replied just as glibly:

"David Copperfield you're not."

My hopes and dreams of becoming a professional singer were dashed. I knew that this damage was irreparable. There was nothing I could do. I would have to live with it. What do you do with your life when the one thing you wanted to do, your purpose for being on this planet is no longer an option?

Since I found out this news, I stopped singing. I can still sing a little bit; I sing for myself, for my kittens, in the house, in the car, wherever I want.

I can change my voice and sound like many singers. If I'm not singing out loud, there is a soundtrack playing in my head.

I thought I was meant to be a singer. I thought that God put me on this planet to sing. Whether in church on Sunday, in a quiet rehearsal room, on a stage, it didn't matter. I thought I was put on this Earth to sing.

But I was wrong.

I have found my voice again, in my writing.

It doesn't fill a church with its resonance or make a crowd applaud.

But I have a voice. It is in my poetry. My poetry is my song.

My song soars through the air, dances among the stars, flies to the moon and back.

I didn't know then what I believe I know now.

I still have a purpose.

I wasn't put on this Earth to sing.

I was put on this Earth to use my voice.

In whatever medium I choose.

The Bigger Picture

Where were You?   December 8, 2012

There are many events in our shared history that seem to mark our lives. When we talk about these events, the common question is, "Where were you?" For example:

**Where were you when John F. Kennedy was shot?
Where were you when you saw the
landing on the moon?
Where were you when
Martin Luther King Jr. was shot?
Where were you when John Lennon was shot?
Where were you when the space ship
Challenger blew up?
Where were you on September 11?**

These questions, and their answers, bring us closer together. I'd like to answer one of these questions now.

I remember this event. I was eight years old; one of my cousins had just died. We traveled to another state for her funeral. It was on a bitterly cold December day. After the funeral we all proceeded outside of the church and waited for her casket to come out of the church. We stood in a line, my family and I, in the freezing cold. I was standing next to my mother. The adults talked amongst themselves; I stood silently. I then remember hearing someone say,

"Did you hear John Lennon was killed?"

An audible gasp rose from the people within earshot. I stood there confused.

"Mom? Who is John Lennon?"

"He's a Beatle dear."

"Oh...........Mom? What's a Beatle?"

The Bigger Picture

I was then told that the Beatles was the name of a rock group from the 1960s. I had only heard John Lennon's name once. I didn't know who he was, who the Beatles were, what John Lennon looked like or sounded like.

I didn't know that he was half of the most influential songwriting team in history.

I didn't know that the Beatles were the most popular musical group on the planet, or that they'd broken up two years before I was born. I didn't even know *how* John Lennon had died.

But I knew from that gasp that I heard that something important had happened that day, and that an important person was gone.

From that day on, I began to try to find out more information on the Beatles. In the days before the internet or CDs or mp3 players, I went to my local library and read about them.

The first time I heard the Beatles music, I didn't know it was them. My sisters had some of their albums, and I began to listen to them.

As I grew, I then knew the Fab Four by name. While other kids my age were listening to Pink Floyd and INXS, I was listening to Sgt. Pepper.

Today is the anniversary of the assassination of John Lennon. His killing was a truly tragic event that reverberated across the universe. I am grateful for the musical legacy he created and for his message of peace. I think the world today still needs to hear that message.

The world still misses you John.

The Bigger Picture

Enough is Enough December 14, 2012

A few months ago I took part in the 100 Thousand Poets for Change. I had many topics to choose from. I decided to write about gun control. There have been several massacres this year in the United States-human beings shooting other human beings. Today in Connecticut two men entered a school and began shooting. At this hour, there are 26 people dead-18 of those dead are children. Children who went to school to get an education-not to be killed. The violence has to stop. We are better than this. I now share with you the poem I wrote for the day of change: "Enough is Enough."

Back on July 20 in Colorado people went to the midnight showing of the latest Hollywood movie to hit the big screen. They went there to see the movie, have a good time. A few minutes into the movie a gunman entered the darkened movie theater and began shooting at the people in the theater.
57 people were wounded, 12 people were killed. The gunman had 3 guns with him in the theater and another gun in his car. The gunman, in riot gear, gas mask, bullet proof vest, was apprehended, and made a comment about his home. It was later found to be booby trapped to ensure the injury or death of anyone entering his residence. He had purchased several hundred rounds of ammunition in the weeks leading up to the event. His youngest murder victim was a 6 year old girl. He has been charged with 24 counts of first degree murder and 116 counts of attempted murder.

On August 5, 16 days later, there was a shooting at a Sikh temple in Wisconsin. They came to the temple to worship.
6 people were killed, many injured. The gunman was killed by police.

Just a few days later, at the Empire State Building in New York City, a gunman killed an ex co-worker of his, and injured 9 people. The gunman was killed by police.

The Bigger Picture

These acts were perpetrated by mentally ill, criminally insane, deeply disturbed men. (I'm sure some other descriptive words can be inserted in that sentence.) I don't know about you, but I am tired about hearing about shootings that have happened on the nightly news.

The Second Amendment to the US Constitution states:
**"A well-regulated militia being necessary
to the security of a free state,
the right of the people to keep and bear arms
shall not be infringed."**

To my understanding, the second amendment gives an individual the right to own a weapon to protect yourself, your family, your home, if you so choose. It also gives you the right to own a weapon to hunt for food to feed your family.

I believe in this right, and if you chose to own a firearm, I respect your right to do so.

But it must be recognized that this amendment does not give anyone to permission to shoot people in cold blood.

People are being killed in our country, around the world, every day. When is it going to be enough? We need better gun control in this country. As a country, as a people, as citizens of the world, we are better than this.

I do not have the answers; I do not have the solutions. I don't have a magic formula to solve this problem. However I do believe that we need an open dialogue in this country, throughout the world, to ensure that no more innocent lives will be taken.

We have to stop the killing. Enough is enough.

The Bigger Picture

'Tis the Season   December 18, 2012

Christmas is right around the corner.

People are stressed out, tensions are running high.

I work in customer service, so I can tell you this first hand.

People are yelling at one another, tempers are short.

Misunderstandings turn into shouting matches, simple interactions become incidents.

In the season of peace and love, often times it proves to be anything but.

If you find yourself stressed out, take a moment.

Relax.

Breathe.

Count to ten.

Go have a moment to yourself.

Drink a cup of hot chocolate.

Whatever it will take to get you in a peaceful mindset, do it.

Then interact with the world. You'll be glad you did.

Try to keep the meaning of the season in your head if not in your heart-it's a season of love.

Judgment   December 19, 2012

Today I caught myself making a judgment. That is not something I like to admit. It is not a good color on me. Or anyone. Today I overheard someone talking about how they went to a local establishment, and would be patronizing this establishment during the holidays. I thought to myself about what that person had said.

> "Why would he do that? Doesn't he know that that establishment's corporate policies are homophobic? How could he patronize that establishment?"

That's when I caught myself making a judgment. I'm not a racist, I'm not homophobic. I don't judge anyone on their size, skin color, sexual orientation, political alignments, religion or lack thereof. But, naturally, there are some things that happen in the world that I don't agree with. When I heard that person make that statement, it didn't make them immoral, I just didn't happen to agree with his choice of patronizing that establishment. So yes, I judged someone. I'm not proud of it. Does that make me an awful person? No. It makes me human. We are human beings and we judge. Like it or not, we judge. We judge one another all the time:

> **"Look at her eat. She is so fat."**
> **"That hairstyle is so gay." "That was so retarded."**
> **"They need to learn to speak English."**
> **"She is so thin. I bet she goes home and throws up her dinner."**

We make judgments on how people are dressed, people's hairstyle, their behavior, any number of things. Sadly, more often than that, we turn these judgments inward, on ourselves. Our judgments do not serve any purpose. Now that I am aware of it, I realize that I have work to do on banishing all judgments. Just like the rest of us. After all, everyone matters.

The Bigger Picture

Writing a Book   December 27, 2012

Writing a book seems like the easiest thing in the world. "I'm writing a book." Such an easy thing to say. Not an easy thing to actually do. In addition to publishing my poetry in 2013 I am writing a book. I hope to have it completed by this time next year and have it ready to sell in 2014.

I am finding that writing a book is not the easiest thing in the world. In fact, for me, I'm finding it very difficult.

I know the story I want to tell:
"Girl meets boy, boy meets girl, boy changes girl's life forever."

However actually telling the story is proving to be a tedious task.

I have never written a book before, and have never written a story before. I know the story, I know how I want to tell it, I know what I want to convey. But actually getting from point "A" to point "B" is quite the challenge.

I find myself getting lost in the dialogue. It can be very confining and tedious. I also find that every writer's friends, "Criticism" and "Doubt" are at every corner. I just have to tell the story. I'll critique it and clean it up after it is written.

If I get this done, if I write the book, tell the story I wanted to tell and publish it, it will be the most daunting achievement of my literary career. As a good friend told me, "It doesn't matter when you finish the book, just finish it."

> *"There is nothing to writing. All you do is sit down at a typewriter and bleed."*
> *-Ernest Hemingway*

The Bigger Picture

Lessons from 2012   December 30, 2012

With the approach of a new year, it is common to think back on the past year, what we've experienced, what we've gone through, what we've endured, what we've survived, what we've learned.

I have learned many things this year. Here is some of what I have learned:

I learned that:
- It's fun to think and dream about the next year, and all the future holds
- It's fun to get your name mentioned on the radio
- I want another chance to celebrate my milestone birthday.
- I want to do it all over again, in a foreign city.
- Pinterest is awesome!
- Although I hate sports, I loved watching the Olympics
- I am addicted to a certain caramel drink at an International coffee chain
- It's not the end of the world if you didn't get the job. It wasn't meant to be. Something better is waiting.
- I have the capacity to be selfless
- I could be compassionate in helping a cherished pet out of her misery
- I could be there with my pet as her soul left this Earth
- There is one more star in the sky
- We should keep our expectations of others low. If people don't do what they promised, we can't be disappointed.
- Whatever the future holds, it all depends on me
- I want to self-publish my poetry and book
- I want to create my own publishing company
- Unconditional anything doesn't exist
- If something seems too good to be true, it probably is

The Bigger Picture

I have growing intolerance and impatience for
    dishonesty and lies
Lies translate into any language
The truth hurts most when it is after a lie
I can survive being hurt and publicly humiliated by my
    "best friend"
I can survive what was done to me on purpose
I can walk away from my "best friend"
If someone swears that they will never hurt you-
    be ready. They will.
Anyone who would treat me like that is not a true
    friend
Games are things best played on a board, not with
    people's lives
I would rather be alone than abused and played
We can only know someone by what they chose to show
    us
Words can be heavy things, like rocks. They can be full
    of sentiment and love and meaning.
Words can be light things, like feathers floating in the
    wind. They can be empty, devoid of any sentiment or
    love or meaning
The phrase "I Love You" should be used sparingly. It
    should only be said if and when it is really meant.
I am not the same person that I was at the beginning of
    the year
No one else can have my power
When you know better you do better
I KnoW more
I am the keeper of the key to my heart
I can fly again
I can see the bigger picture
To move on I need to forgive
That person doesn't deserve my forgiveness. But I do.
As old friendships die, new ones are born

Two little kittens can bring so much light and love into your life
Everyone matters
It is amazing to be featured on the same website as a Beatle
I am tired of hearing about massacres due to gun violence in the US. Gun control is needed now. We are better than this. Enough is enough.
I no longer play to an audience of one
Change can be a good thing
Music legends die. Their music changed our lives, our world, forever. And life goes on.
We are given a blank page to write our stories every day
We are the authors of our own stories
I am an artist
I still have a voice
I am beautiful whether you tell me I am or not
There is a wonderful and welcoming community of silence
Building a website and transferring a domain name is not as easy as 1-2-3
Writing a book is not the easiest task to endeavor
I have an amazing support system of family and friends who are there for me for every success
I have reserves of strength I didn't know I had

The past year was full of ups and downs, many challenges, elation and devastation, laughter and heartaches.

But I have grown and survived. I am stronger than ever. I am flying again.

My wings are healing and are getting stronger than ever.

It feels good to feel the wind under my wings. Just watch me fly.

The Bigger Picture

My Story   January 4, 2013

I began this blog a month ago. I thought it might be a nice time to talk about how I got here.

My pen name is Esperanza Habla. This is not my real name. I am an American and I work in a library.

As I became active in social media, I began to acquire friends in different countries, several of whom spoke Spanish. I then decided to teach myself Spanish, to communicate with these friends and to strengthen my language skills. (I had taken some Spanish in school and remembered some vocabulary, but very little else.)

Around the same time, a group of these friends encouraged me to use poetry to express myself, what I was thinking and feeling. I shared my writing with these friends, in English. I then shared the writing with more friends-friends who only spoke Spanish. I continued to hone my skills in Spanish through my writing.

The more I shared my writing with this core group of friends, the more positive feedback I got. They encouraged me to continue writing and to never stop. I soon found myself with many poems I had written. I then decided to create a blog.

I was still very insecure in my writing and couldn't write under my real name. I decided on Esperanza Habla because, translated into English, it means "Hope Speaks." I think hope should speak. And I certainly have a lot to say.

In March of 2011 I created the blog, the "Words of Hope." It is a bilingual blog, with poems in English and Spanish. It has been a great success, attracting over 6,000 readers in over 20 countries.

The Bigger Picture

As I mentioned earlier, I launched this blog on December 1. I began this blog to expand my poetry to new readers. People can come to this blog and chose their language. The blog is then translated into your language. There are over 60 languages to choose from.

To date I have had over 1,400 visitors. I wanted a successful launch of this blog, and I got it. Everyone is welcome and there are no language barriers, or barriers of any sort.

Another aspect of my learning Spanish has been a new career as a translator. I have translated written works from Spanish and Castilian into English for authors around the world. I will soon begin a new translation project in French.

Over the course of my growth as a writer, a friend pointed out that my writing has, and that I have, an "indigo" quality. I didn't understand what that person meant. I looked up the traits of being "indigo.' The traits of being an indigo person means that they are:
Wise, insightful, spiritually aware, intuitive, perceptive, devoted, just, fair, responsible, and devoted to the truth.

At first I thought this person was insane to say this to me. I didn't see myself as being indigo at all. I now strongly identify myself with being indigo. It has been my favorite color for some time-now I know why. I am an indigo poet.

The other quality of my writing, or my literary career, is the moon. I have a strong tie to the moon. I share this tie with my friends in foreign lands. As I once wrote on this blog, a friend once told me:

The Bigger Picture

"If you miss me, if you need me, look to the moon. We're under the same moon. Look to the moon. I'm there waiting for you. You're not alone."

The moon is a friend, an inspiration, a constant companion.

The New Year has arrived and I have many things I want to accomplish.

I want to create my own publishing company.

I want to also publish two books of my poetry to date:

"I am Hope" and "Just Me."

The world is wide open. Anything I can dream I can accomplish.

I want to thank those friends, A, C, L, S for reading my first writings and encouraging me to write more. Without their encouragement I would not be a writer today.

I would not be the woman, the person I am today.

Thank you to all my friends and family for your endless encouragement.

Thank you too to all of my readers. I am grateful for your support of my work.

I am an indigo poet. I am the poet of the moon. I am the Indigo Poet of the Moon. I write whenever inspiration strikes. Whenever I hear the muse.

So that is my story. What's yours?

The Bigger Picture

Indigo Colored Glasses January 4, 2013

There is an expression here in the US to look at something "through rose colored glasses."

This means that a person is looking at things in a positive way, or seeing things in a way that is contrary to reality, whether positive or negative.

I have a different set of glasses.

My glasses are not rose colored, they are indigo.

I am an indigo poet, an indigo person, so it makes sense that I would have indigo glasses.

For me, my indigo glasses give me clarity. I notice the world as it passes me by.

The things I see become thoughts that swirl around in my head for days, eventually coming to rest in the form of a poem.

I received my indigo colored glasses some time ago.

With these glasses I have a much clearer vision.

I see the world, myself in the world, the biggest vistas, the smallest details.

I see things as they are.

From my truth. My reality.

Through my indigo colored glasses.

The Bigger Picture

Meetings and Partings   January 5, 2013

I had a ghost from my past write me a note the other day. I knew this person was going to write me. Don't ask me how. I knew this person was going to write me. I am glad this person wrote me. It confirmed to me that, although it was terribly painful, our friendship ending was for the best and absolutely the right thing. Months have passed; I can see their side of things, and I think they can now see mine. But again, my not being friends with this person is for the best. These people are called ghosts from our past for a reason-because the end of the friendship, relationship, partnership, can haunt us. It is that way for all of us-friends come in and out of our lives at the drop of the hat. People transfer schools, change jobs, lose touch, walk away purposely, and sometimes, sadly, die. The people in your life now, they are in your life for a reason. They are teaching you something, showing you something that the universe needs for you to know. Likewise you too are teaching them something, showing them something they need to know. These friends and lovers are in your life for a certain time. The people who aren't in your life anymore, there is a reason for that. You taught them everything they needed to know. And they did the same for you. The end of a friendship or relationship can be excruciatingly painful.

In times like these, it is wise to take your time and heal from the experience. Look at the good things that happened from the friendship. Learn to look at the bigger picture. Listen to the universe. Learn the lessons that the experience taught you. Pray that the other person learned the lessons they were meant to learn. Begin the slow and agonizing process of forgiveness. There was a reason the two of you met. And there's a reason that it's over.

> *"Life is made up of meetings and partings.*
> *That is the way of it."*
> -Kermit the Frog-Muppet Christmas Carol

The Bigger Picture

Old Friends　　　　　　　January 15, 2013

In addition to my poetry, I am also writing my first novel-
"Samantha". It's about the usual thing-
"girl meets boy, boy meets girl, boy changes her life forever."

I have been working on formatting my poetry to sell, and creating my new business, and writing poetry.

I haven't written anything for the book in nearly a month. Until yesterday.

It was foreign at first, going back to the story, finding the scene, remembering what I wanted to occur in the scene. Within a few minutes, I was back to the story and writing with ease.

It felt good to go back, to be creative, to tell this story, to meet up with these characters again.

This may be a unique thing, something that only writers experience. For those who do not write, this may be a hard concept to grasp-why it would feel good to be back amongst these characters that you yourself have created.

I can only liken it to visiting your old neighborhood- experiencing the different sights and sounds, going back to a restaurant you used to go to and having your favorite meal.

Or, hearing a song you'd forgotten about on the radio; upon hearing it again you are transported to a specific time and place or life event.

It's a feeling of the familiar, of comfort.

Like meeting up with old friends.

The Bigger Picture

Gratitude   January 17, 2013

One of the things that we as human beings need to work on, need to acquire the skill of, is gratitude. I've seen some inspirational videos lately, talking about the concept of gratitude and how we need to be grateful for what we have.

I thought about this, and I am grateful for what I have. I have a job, I am able to pay my bills and have a little money left over, I have my own home, a vehicle, two adorable kittens, my health, modern conveniences in my home-electricity, running water, Wi-Fi, a group of faithful friends and a family that loves me. But, that is not all I'm grateful for. I'm also grateful for some things I don't have.

This might be a strange concept. Think about it-there are so many things that we do have, and should be grateful for. But there are also things in our life that we don't have. We should be grateful for those things as well. For example:

I don't live in a part of the world where water is unavailable
    to me.
I don't have a crippling mortgage.
I don't live in a dangerous area.
My house wasn't swept away in a hurricane.
I am not in an abusive relationship-physically or spiritually.
I don't have people in my life who are unsupportive of me.
I don't live in fear.

When I am alone, in the solitude of thought, when I think of what I am grateful for, I think of all the blessings in my life, the things I have, and, as equally important, the things I don't.

The Bigger Picture

Living History   January 21, 2013

Today in the United States we celebrate the life and work of Dr. Martin Luther King Jr. This is always a day to sit back and reflect on his life, his work. The country is now a dramatically different place. That is greatly thanks to him. He is proof that one person can make a difference.

Today is also significant for another reason-President Barack Obama is having his second inauguration. On the national day of recognizing Dr. Martin Luther King Jr. This is an amazing day in my country. During Obama's first inauguration, I was deeply moved. For the first time in my life, I was proud to be an American. We as a nation had elected the best person for the job. For the first time ever, the person we elected president was a person of color.

I was filled with pride as an American. It seemed that Dr. King's words, vision, had come true...

> ***"I have a dream that my four little children***
> ***will one day live in a nation where they will not be***
> ***judged by the color of their skin,***
> ***but by the content of their character."***
> ***-Martin Luther King, Jr.***

The significance of this day is not lost on me. It should not be lost on anyone. If Obama had lost the last election, yes, we would be swearing someone else in to office. But he didn't. And this day would not carry the immense significance that it does.

If you live in the US, take a moment today. Take a moment to reflect where we were just decades ago. Think about how far we've come in that time, as a people and as a country, in the aspects of racism, poverty, housing, voting rights. Think about how much farther we have to go.

The Bigger Picture

Ode to Inspiration   January 29, 2013

I spoke to an online friend last week; this person is a performer and a writer. I asked how he had been; he said he had been fine. I asked him how his theater festival had gone in the past month; he said it went very well. I then asked him if he had written anything recently. He replied,
"No, inspiration hasn't come yet."

I totally understand that sensation. You can't write about something when you're not inspired. In the past, I have known writers who can sit down and write for 8 hours a day. I don't work that way. I am like my friend; I have to write when inspiration comes. I told my friend, "Inspiration is like love. You can't look for it; it will find you."

I then began to think about inspiration, and about writing. It then occurred to me that, with some exceptions, every piece of music we have ever heard was written. Every piece of dialogue we witness in a play was written. Every nuance of movement on stage has been written. If these things weren't written, they would have been performed once and lost forever. I thought about the story of the muse, the legend of the nine Greek sisters who inspire artists of many varieties.

I don't know if I have a muse that whispers in my ear, giving me thoughts which turn into poetry or not. Inspiration itself may be the muse. Inspiration is like a beautiful butterfly. You can chase it with every ounce of strength you have; chances are it will fly away from you. But if you sit quietly, the butterfly will, more often than not, find you.

If I am silent on this blog, it is not on purpose, and not because I want to be. It's because I am waiting for the muse to whisper in my ear, waiting for the butterfly to find me.

The Bigger Picture

Acts of Kindness   January 31, 2013

So many things happen these days that we often don't take the time to notice the little things. Little things people do for one another. Picking up something and handing it to the person that dropped it. Leaving the door open for a person when you're going out of a store. Stopping to ask if a person is alright after a fall. These actions are often termed "Random Acts of Kindness."

These acts of kindness are a recurring theme in the United States these days. There has been so much gun violence in the last year in this country, so much needless carnage, that people are taking time to stop, notice the little things around them, and to be grateful for their blessings.

In December of last year, there was a mass shooting at an elementary school in the state of Connecticut here in the United States. 26 people were killed in the massacre. 20 of the dead were children. As part of the aftermath of the shooting, people around the US were encouraging people to perform 26 random acts of kindness, one for each person that died that tragic day. I agree that acts of kindness are wonderful things. But they don't have to be random.

I have come up with a plan for my acts of kindness. There are so many organizations in the US, throughout the world, that do acts of kindness for the greater good, every single day of the year. My plan is to support some of those organizations. For every month this year, I will donate to a charity. I will donate a small amount-just $10.00. It is a modest amount, one that will not drain any of my monetary resources, but will help many people.

The Bigger Picture

I have already done my first act of kindness this year. I have purchased products from a fair trade company. The Fair Trade Organization defines a Fair Trade as…

> **"…a trading partnership, based on dialogue, transparency and respect, that seek greater equity in international trade. It contributes to sustainable development by offering better trading conditions to, and securing the rights of, marginalized producers and workers – especially in the South. Fair Trade Organizations, backed by consumers, are engaged actively in supporting producers, awareness raising and in campaigning for changes in the rules and practice of conventional international trade."**
> © World Fair Trade Organization

The products I purchased were made by artisans in Thailand, in a village of over 400 people.

My purchase further encourages fair trade, and helps to give these artisans a living wage and a better life.

All from buying a product from a fair trade company.

The company I purchased the products from had a variety of goods from a myriad of countries around the world.

That is my plan, my act of kindness. I will donate $10 a month to a charity that I believe in, that does a greater good for our planet and for one another.

So what about you? How can you help? What can you contribute to the world? What will your act of kindness be?

The Bigger Picture

Forgiveness February 7, 2013

I have been thinking a lot lately about the concept of forgiveness. I have heard many quotes about forgiveness. People always say, **"Forgive and forget." "Be quick to forgive." "To err is human; to forgive, divine."**

There are many symbols of forgiveness around the world, including the chalice, the dove, the olive branch, a candle, the Christian cross. My favorite symbol of forgiveness is the feather.

Have you ever looked at a feather? Really looked at a feather? There are so many intricacies and complexities in a single feather-the stem, the veins, the texture, the size and shape, the many hues of color. To me, the feather is the perfect symbol of forgiveness. As many complexities there are in a single feather, there are that many complexities to forgiveness.

The act of forgiveness is easier said than done. I am reminded of a quote I heard recently from C. S. Lewis:
> ***"Everyone says forgiveness is a lovely idea,
> until they have something to forgive."***

In our lives we all have hurts, have pain, have been devastated by someone, maybe even violated by someone. I believe that the deeper the hurt, the longer the process of forgiveness takes.

Forgiveness is especially hard when the person has not shown any remorse for their behavior, have not apologized for their actions, when we feel they do not deserve to be forgiven.

However, we need to think of ourselves also, not just the person who wronged us. We need to choose to forgive ourselves as well, for letting that person hurt us.

The Bigger Picture

When someone hurts us, causes us pain, takes advantage of us, we have a choice to forgive. We have a choice to let go and move on. We have a choice to forgive the person that has hurt us.

We also have the choice to forgive the deeds that were done to us. We can forgive the person who hurt us and not what they did.

Likewise we can forgive what that person did to us and never forgive them.

The act of forgiveness is often seen as excusing the behavior of the person who wronged you or hurt you.

In reality, forgiveness is really a gift to yourself. You're letting go of the pain, the hurt, moving on, and obtaining peace.

The act of forgiveness is a choice. It takes time to heal. You're going to feel how you feel until you stop feeling that way.
You can't rush it, you can't hurry it along, you can't ignore it.

Be open to the choice of forgiveness, be it for the person or what they did to you.

Be open to forgiveness. It is never easy. Take control of the situation and when you are ready, choose to forgive that person for all that they did to you.

Or, choose to forgive their actions. Pray that they learn the lessons they need to learn. And, most importantly, forgive yourself for letting a person you truly cared about hurt you so deeply.

Relax. Breathe. Forgive.

The Bigger Picture

The Gift of the Moon   February 9, 2013

This week I had the opportunity to reunite with family that lives thousands of miles away. As part of our visit, we had "Christmas Part 2." We couldn't all be together at Christmas, and this was a chance to get together; while we had the chance, we had a mini second Christmas. There were many gifts that were too fragile to send through the mail. We knew we would be getting together as a family this week, so we decided to wait.

This year for Christmas we had drawn names of who to get a gift for. This year my nephew had my name. I didn't know what I would receive. I had no expectations.

For me, giving a gift is much more important than getting one. I like to put much thought into the gift I am giving; making sure the gift is perfect for that person.

To my surprise, I received a beautiful framed photograph of the moon-that my nephew himself had taken. I have never seen such an image of the moon before. A perfect photo of the moon. The perfect present for me.

The gift of the moon. The moon
is my inspiration, my comfort,
my companion, my muse.
The perfect present for
the poet of the moon.

Behold my friend,
my inspiration, my muse,
the moon.

Thank you David.

The Bigger Picture

Dedication February 12, 2013

Being a poet, being a part of a vast artistic community, I have met artists of all types. Performers of many genres-dancers, performance artists, mimes, clowns, contortionists, jugglers, magicians, musicians, disk jockeys.

I have also met many writers, poets, authors, playwrights. The various fields of these artists are as varied as the artists themselves.

However, there are some things that these artists have in common-passion for their art form. Perseverance.

Perhaps the greatest trait that all of these artists have in common-dedication.

Dedication to learn something new.

Dedication to perform their art to the best of their abilities.

Dedication to rehearse and refine their skills until it is perfect.

Dedication to their craft. To be the best they can be.

I have known authors who can sit at a desk with a computer, or pen and paper, and write for 8 hours straight.

I have known performance artists that need to exercise for multiple hours a day just to stay in top physical condition.

I have known performers to train and rehearse for hours to get a performance piece right.

I have known artists that constantly go to classes to learn new things to enhance their craft.

The Bigger Picture

Last week I spoke to a fellow artist. During the course of our conversation, the person said that they were a bit sore.

I asked this person if they had had a strenuous rehearsal that day, or a grueling exercise routine.

This person told me that they had gone to a workshop to learn a new skill to perform, to add to their repertoire; but, that was not why they were sore.

They were tired and sore because they had walked to the workshop.

The location of the workshop was over 90 minutes away from their house.

They had walked to the workshop. More than 90 minutes away.

Sitting at a computer and writing for 8 hours a day.

Exercising for 4 or more hours a day to stay in top physical fitness.

Rehearsing for hours on end to get everything right.

Walking to a workshop 90 minutes away from home.

That is dedication.

The Bigger Picture

The Smiling Moon February 13, 2013

Did you see it last night? I had never seen it before. It was an amazing sight to see.

Last night, after work, I was walking out to my car. I looked up in the sky to see if I could spot the moon. I never know if she's in a half moon, crescent moon, or in a full moon. My personal favorite is when the moon is full, and we can see her moonlight and radiance shine throughout the dark night sky.

But when I looked at the moon, I saw something I have never seen before. It was a crescent moon; however, it wasn't your ordinary every day crescent moon. I had never seen a stage of the moon like it before.

Normally, when you see a crescent moon, you see just a sliver of the moon, on the side of the moon. However, that's not what I saw last night. I saw a crescent moon, but on the bottom of the moon. It was the most bizarre sight to see. I had never seen anything like that before in my life.

I stopped a moment to really look at what I was seeing, a crescent moon at the bottom of the moon. It was then that it struck me. The moon was smiling.

I have seen some depictions of this phenomenon online; it has been likened to the Cheshire Cat from Alice in Wonderland. To me it was more of a smile, coy and timid, knowing and assuring, almost like that of the Mona Lisa.

You can compare it to anything you want. To me it was my dear friend, the moon, saying hello, sending me a smile.

So...did you see it last night?

The Bigger Picture

Trust　　　　　　　　February 19, 2013

The other day I was approached by an online friend-he was upset and needed to talk. I wrote this person and asked what was wrong. He then stated that he had just broken up with his girlfriend. It was obvious that he needed to talk about it, and I was more than happy to let him talk.

This young man asked me many questions, most of which were on the topic of how to recover from a broken heart. I told him that we have all been rejected, and we have all had a broken heart. He then asked me a profound question:
"How do you trust again?"

To me, that was a deeply profound question. At first, I wasn't sure how he meant it. I wasn't sure if he was asking how he could trust the person that had broken his heart; I also wondered if he was asking how to trust in people again, since he had just had such a heart breaking experience. I began telling him a quote I had recently heard online:
"Trust is like a crumpled up piece of paper.
Once it has been crumpled up,
it will never be the same again."

I told him what I believe, and how I look at trust. Yes, I have had a friend lie to me, treat me like dirt and break my heart. But, that experience has not made me recoil into a shell and not talk to anyone. I conduct myself as I always have. I am truthful with my friends.

To answer the question,
"How do you trust someone again who has hurt you?"

I don't have an answer for that question. I don't think I could ever trust someone that hurt me that deeply ever again.

The Bigger Picture

But, to answer the question,
"How do you trust again?"

For me, it was easy. Other people didn't hurt me; it was just that one person.

I still believe in people. I believe in the good in people.

I have learned to not expect much from other people.

If they don't live up to their promises, I can't be disappointed.

Be open to possibilities.

Guard yourself to protect yourself when needed.

Be willing to trust.

But, at the same time, do not trust blindly.

Don't punish your friends or family or the world for something one person did.

Pray for that person; let the hurt go.

Be open to trust.

The Bigger Picture

The Adventures of Kit and Caboodle   February 20, 2013

I lay in bed as I begin to wake. Consciousness leads to a stream of thought. I open my eyes. I see that it is still night time-or very early morning. I decide to go unconscious again. Just then a cat leaps on to my bed, using my pillow as a trampoline to bounce to their end target-the windowsill behind my bed. *Well I'm awake*, I think to myself.

That was just one of many curious happenings in my home since I have adopted two little kittens, Kit and Caboodle. (Those are not their real names. I am calling them by these names to protect their identities.) I adopted the kittens several months ago from a local animal shelter. I feel good knowing I rescued two kittens from a bleak fate. In the months that they have been in my home they have filled it with laughter and light and love.

The two kittens are not from the same litter; however, I brought them home the same day, and the two have bonded together as if they were sisters. They play together, groom each other, even cuddle up to sleep together. It is very precious to see them interact with one another.

As we all have bonded, we have come to know one another and our preferences. Each kitten has their favorite place to sit, to be held, not held, to sit on my lap, to sit beside me, etc. Personally, I've had to learn how adapt to having cats with claws. (There have been a few moments of accidental bloodletting.)

As every kitten that I have ever known, they are just little balls of kitten energy. My sleep has been disrupted ever since I brought them home. With all of their kitty mischief that they get into, which is frustrating and, thankfully rare, there are deeply cute moments as well.

The Bigger Picture

It has been very precious to me to see the things they have learned from one another; it is very funny to see a kitten do a behavior that I only knew the other kitten to do. Using my pillow as a trampoline to have a prime spot to stare out the window is a rare occurrence.

The days are filled with kittens romping through the house, sleeping closely together after a long morning of play.

The nights are filled with exuberant play until we all go to bed.

As I have written before, everyone has their own story.

We are given a blank page every day, and we are the authors of our own stories.

It seems that I now have two stories. The first is my own story of growth and purpose as a poet, a person and a woman.

The second story is that of being caregiver to my kittens. It is called, "The Adventures of Kit and Caboodle."

The cats known as Kit and Caboodle

Building a Legacy   February 23, 2013

I have been working for several weeks now on my books of poetry. I will have two books in English and two books in Spanish: "I am Hope" and "The Bigger Picture."

The poetry in the books will be from this blog, as well as my first blog, the Words of Hope.

www.esperanzahabla.blogspot.com

However, in going through my poetry over the last three years, I found that there are many poems that never made it to the blog.

Some were too personal, some were written for a particular person, some I didn't think good enough to publish.

I've since had a change of heart. Everything will be going in the books.

It has been very interesting for me, compiling these works, getting everything together, in the order in which it was written.

I like to do that, to read poetry, books in the order in which they were written, listen to music in the order in which it was written. Through this you can see (and hear) the evolution of the artist in their craft.

Going through my reserves of poetry has been a very eye opening experience for me, as well as a mind opening one. I read a poem and remember what I thought, why I said what I said, why I wrote what I wrote, who I wrote a poem to, why I felt what I felt.

The Bigger Picture

I also took a moment to think about where I began, how I started as a poet, how far I've come, how much I've grown, and how my poetry has gained an audience. I've had readers from over 30 countries read my words. That is astonishing to me.

When I began to write, it was a means to express myself.

I sent the poems to a couple of friends.

I never thought that anyone else, or that the world, would care to read anything I had to say.

I have grown a lot in the last three years, as an artist, a person and a woman.

Working on the poetry, thinking about all of these things is a nice period of reflection.

That's how I see it, reflection. But, that is one way to look at it.

As my good author/publisher/mentor friend said to me today:
"You're building a legacy. Your stuff will be here long after you are gone."

I had never thought about that before.

My poetry will live on.

Long after I've left.

That is a daunting thought.

But, not when in the context of building a legacy.

A Life of Words

February 27, 2013

I live a life of words. This may not come as a surprise to you, because I am a poet. But it surprised me. I began my life as a poet three years ago. But I have been surrounded by words long before that. As a three year old child I read words from books. As a young child I learned to sing words in song. As a youth I read words in study. I have worked in a library for over a decade. Libraries are such sacred spaces. Libraries are sanctuaries of words. My library has close to 60,000 books in it. Every book, be it a novel, an instructional book, a self-help book, a foreign language manual, every book is filled with words. Every book contains someone's story. Libraries are cavernous formations of words. Just imagine the vast resources. Everyone has a story to tell. You might find it appropriate that I work in a library, because I am a poet. You might find it ironic. The irony didn't occur to me until recently.

I am surrounded by words. I have words in my head all the time; usually the words are lyrics from a favorite song. Or, the words are thoughts which will later morph into poetry that you will read. I am surrounded by words. I am enveloped in words. They are my constant companions. They are the colors in my palette. I live a life of words.

"To get the right word in the right place is a rare achievement. To condense the diffused light of a page of thought into the luminous flash of a single sentence, is worthy to rank as a prize composition just by itself...Anybody can have ideas--the difficulty is to express them without squandering a quire of paper on an idea that ought to be reduced to one glittering paragraph."
- Mark Twain

The Bigger Picture

The Journey　　　　　　　　　　March 4, 2013

Over the past month I have been gathering my poetry to put into book form. The poetry begins with my unsure, hesitant, insecure scratchings with pen and paper. The poetry transforms, evolves over the course of my body of work. And so do I.

I began writing three years ago with the encouragement of a few friends. Being writers themselves, they were profoundly generous with their time and in giving me their thoughts and opinions about what I had written.

I was very insecure when I began. I had no idea I had any talent as a writer. I thought that my writings were just scribblings, expressing my thoughts and emotions. When they said that they liked what I had written, I thought they were just being nice. Little did I know at the time that I had embarked on a path of reflection, clarity and awareness that would change my life forever.

If someone had told me five years ago that I would become a poet, I would have thought they were insane. If anyone had told me that I would start my own publishing house and publish my poetry, I would have laughed in their face.

As a writer, I write a poem, post it, and share it. It has been said that the Internet is the trash dump for the common man, that it gives every idiot a stage to express their opinions. For me it has given me a platform, a voice, and an audience.

I am grateful that I have an audience and that you are indeed listening. I am humbled to hear when something I have written has helped someone. That is profoundly moving to hear.

The Bigger Picture

As I have compiled my poetry together I have taken time to look back on what I have gone through, and what I have learned. Some of my lessons were easy. Most of them were not.

I am thankful to God, the higher power, the universe for teaching me the lessons I needed to learn, about trust, honesty, boundaries, expectations, forgiveness, love.

I have grown as an artist, as a woman and as a person in these last three years.

I have evolved into the person I am destined to be.

I have a new clarity, a new understanding, a new honesty, a new purpose.

Thank you for accompanying me on my journey and being there for me in my darkest hours.

Help keep me mindful of what I have learned.

Help me continue on my path of awareness and clarity.

Guide me on my path and teach me the lessons I have yet to learn.

This has been an amazing journey.

A humbling, exhilarating, painful, joyous, humiliating, eye opening, heart breaking, breathtaking, devastating, amazing journey.

I will remember this time in my life forever.

Thank you for sharing it with me.

The Bigger Picture

Poetry   March 6, 2013

It should come as no surprise that I have a passion for poetry. I write whenever inspiration comes. I have read poetry of many famous poets. However, I find the most inspiration from my contemporaries. Last night I had the pleasure to read poetry from an online friend. This person has written for years, and doesn't have a blog of his writings. His words were filled with passion and power. They leapt of the page, soaring into the clouds.

After reading some of this person's poetry, I encouraged this person to begin a blog of his writings. He remarked that maybe a blog should be in English, so more people could read his work.

I then told him that he could make a blog like this one, where the reader can choose their own language. There are over 60 languages to choose from. Language doesn't have to be a barrier. My friend loved this suggestion. Reading the words of this online friend, reading their poetry, it reaffirms my love of this art form. It makes me want to continue on my path. To write more. To be better.

Poetry is all around us. It's in the poems we write, of course, but also in the lyrics of a song, the movement of a body in a dance, a performance of a concerto for instruments, in the colors on an artist's canvas, in the flight of a butterfly. Poetry is everywhere. You just have to look for it.

"Poetry is the music of the soul"-Voltaire

"People have been writing poetry for you before you were born. We are in a place where we need to use and seize poetry. All of it was made for us."
-Maya Angelou

The Bigger Picture

Loss March 12, 2013

In the past month, I have noticed an unfortunate turn of events. One of my co-workers lost a loved one. An online friend broke up with their boyfriend of over a decade. Another co-worker lost a loved one. A friend's fiancé died-they had been engaged ten years. You might be asking yourself what these incidents have in common. The answer is simple-loss.

The subject of loss is one that I am familiar with. My cherished cat of seventeen years died last year. Also last year I lost my best friend-not to death, to life.

Losses in life can be devastating things. They can send us into a spiral of pain and despair that can take months if not years to overcome.

In the past month some of these friends who have experienced losses, or had family members who experienced the loss, have come to me and asked me for help. Even though the circumstances were different, there are some common phrases:
> **"I don't know what to do." "What should I do?"
> "Tell me what to do."**

Quite often we ask for something to do in these situations because we feel helpless. We feel out of control. We can't take away the pain. We feel helpless when we see a family member in despair. Our own pain makes us want to fall to our knees and collapse in a puddle of tears and hurt.

One of my good friends came to me after having her heart broken.
> **"What do I do? I don't know what to do."**

The Bigger Picture

My answer to her was to relax, breathe, read, pray, eat some chocolate, be good to herself, ride the waves of emotion as they come. If you have experienced a loss, I do not need to tell you how painful it can be.

One thing that I cannot stress enough is "be good to yourself."

Surround yourself in positive thoughts, things that make you comfortable-a cup of tea, a long hot bath.

Take the emotions as they come. Find someone to talk to.

If the loss you are feeling is centered around a specific person, look at the bigger picture. Don't concentrate on the end.

Be grateful for the good things that happened while this person was in your life. Think about everything you learned from the experience.

Write down what you cannot say, what you wish you could have said, what you want to say. Every day the hurt gets less and less.

One day you will wake up and something will have changed. It's an indescribable thing, an intangible thing; but you will notice the difference. You will wake up and the hurt won't be as bad anymore.

When I heard this I thought it sounded like a stupid cliché. Trust me when I tell you that this is true.

For those whose friends or loved ones have experienced a loss, my advice would be to relax, breathe, pray, and offer guidance when needed.

The number one thing would be to listen. They need to talk about what they're feeling and experiencing. If you can, let them talk to you. Listen.

Be open to what they are telling you. Pray for them and take care of yourself. You will need to keep up your reserves of strength if they need to lean on you. Keep up your reserves of strength so you can be strong for them. Be willing to listen and offer advice.

If the person needs some time apart, time alone to reflect and deal with their pain, give them that time alone. They will come to you when they are ready.

There are many intense, painful emotions that accompany loss.

The good part about loss is that the hurt is temporary.

It may not feel like it when we're in the middle of it. Trust me, it is only for now.

Everything is only for now. The pain dulls. The scars heal.

One day, very soon, you will awaken and be changed-for the better. The skies will be sunny and the pain won't be as deep.

You will notice that the scars will remain with you as a reminder of what you have gone through, a battle scar signifying what you have survived.

Our scars make us who we are. Our scars make us beautiful.

The Bigger Picture

Infinite Possibilities   March 19, 2013

I have been thinking of late about writers, and what their role is. Also, what their talents are, or powers. Many people who are performers are writers.

Every movement on stage has been written. Every note that is sung has been written. Every word in a soliloquy has been written.

I have also been thinking about writers who write poems, books, stories.

I recently discovered, or realized, that writers have the keys to the universe. We can make anything happen. There are infinite possibilities.

We can create a universe. We can resurrect ancient Babylonians. We can make a fish fly, a bird swim. We can make a rainbow laugh, a mountain weep. We can make it rain upside down. We can make it snow. We can have that last conversation with our loved one in heaven. We can make the invisible visible. We can make the moon sing.

Some might think that this makes writers godlike. I don't believe that. I believe that the imagination is our creative toolbox, a treasure chest holding everything we might ever need. The only limits to our creativity are the limits of our imagination.

I am currently in the middle of writing my own novel. It makes me wonder what other stories I have to tell. When I am ready, I will go to my treasure chest, see what marvelous things I find there. There are infinite possibilities.

The Bigger Picture

My Dear Sally   March 30, 2013

Hello dear friend. I haven't been able to talk to you for a while now. How are you? I am doing well. I have missed you so much Sally. I am sure that there were many things I didn't get to know about you; now I will never have the chance. But, I'm sure there are things that you never knew about me.

For example, I have a weird brain for dates. I remember when certain things happened. I can tell you the day I met E. I can tell you when M told me the truth and came out. I can tell you the day S and I met. I can also tell you when my friendship with him ended.

I remember today, Sally. I remember that you left us two years ago. Today. So much has happened since I saw you last.
I remember going to the hospital to see you. That would be the last time I would see you. And I knew it. I was sorry I couldn't see you towards the end.

I remember I was at work when we got the call. They called me in to the office, to give me some privacy, to tell me you had died. I remember feeling upset at hearing the news.

But, I knew your health was failing. I knew the unfortunate truth, that it was only a matter of time before the cancer took you from us. It wasn't until I went home that night that the reality of the situation hit me.

Do you remember me talking to you that night? I remember that like it was yesterday. I remember going home and having a moment of prayer, and talking to you. I know you heard me that night. Thank you for bringing me solace. I remember going to your viewing. I remember going there with A. There were so many people there Sally. I'm sure you were looking down on us and smiling.

The Bigger Picture

I remember taking photos, to have for myself. I remember the large television they had with the slideshow of your photos. They had so many photos of you they had giant poster boards full!

I remember talking to your husband. He actually remembered who I was. He said that the cards and letters I sent you every week made you feel so good. I was glad to hear that.

I remember seeing you, lying in your casket, which was covered in sunflowers. That flower will always be your flower.

I think I last spoke to you a year ago. So much has happened since then. As I alluded to earlier, S and I parted ways. We were good friends, and we truly loved one another as friends. But, he was not the man I knew him to be.

The person I knew, he genuinely cared for me as a friend, and I know he cared for you. He wrote you that lovely poem that night, when you died. Thank you for drying my tears in his stead.

I cannot tell you what happened with he and I. The end of our friendship was ugly and painful and devastating and humiliating. That being said, it was for the best that it ended. I wish him the best, creatively, artistically. He has so much to give to the world. And to the moon.

Also, last year, my cat Calypso died. It was time for her to go. I had a veterinarian come to my home to have her put to sleep. It was the best thing for her. This wasn't for me, it was solely for her.

That day I knew what was coming, and it upset me deeply. When she passed, it was truly the most precious thing in my life. When she died, it was just peace. No whine, no howls of pain, just solace, peace.

She became energy, light. Like you did. Having the doctor come to send her to heaven was the most selfless thing I have ever done. After that I was not upset. It was over. She found peace. And so did I.

My writing is really taking off. I launched a new blog last December. Sally, you wouldn't believe it. I've had over 4,600 people come to my blog since December! I'm getting 1,200 visits a month! I never did that well on my old blog.

I began writing to express what I was feeling. I never dreamt that I would share those writings with anyone, let alone start a blog.

I am amazed and humbled that people around the world are reading my words. I have decided that I want to publish my poetry. I thought about it, and decided that the best way to do it is to create my own publishing company. I know, I can't believe it either! Who would think that about me? Esperanza-entrepreneur!

Speaking of writing, S published his book. He published it. I'm so proud to know that he published it. It is such an honor to know that I inspired him to write it. I bought a copy, as a keepsake.

Well, I bought two-one for myself and one for Mr. C. I looked in the back of the book-S did mention you. Thank you so much for helping him write it.

Geez Sally, looking back on this letter, you probably already know all of what I just told you. From your vantage point in

The Bigger Picture

the moon, you can see everything that is going on. You can probably see what is yet to come as well.

It feels so good to talk to you again Sally. I have missed you so much.

It's funny, I still have your last message to me on my answering machine. I can't bear to delete it.

I think of you every time I see the photo of that famous author- you look so much like her. Every time I see her photo on one of her books, I think to myself, *that's my Sally*.

Thank you for coming to my window last night. I remember lying in bed, trying to get to sleep, when all of a sudden the room was awash with light. I looked out the window, and I saw you, on the moon, at my window.

Thank you for bringing the moon to me, and for shining your beautiful light, to comfort me. I think of you as my guardian angel. Thank you for watching over me.

I truly miss you Sally. I miss your smile, your laugh.

I have learned so much from you.

I am not alone. There are many people who miss you.

You were a dear friend to me.

You hold a special place in my heart.

Take care my dear Sally. Until next time.

The Bigger Picture

RespectApril 4, 2013

In the past week, there were two court cases brought before the United States Supreme Court, having to do with equal rights. More specifically, these cases were about legally recognizing marriages on a federal level for homosexuals, a right currently only afforded to heterosexuals. These cases appearing before the court created a dialogue in the US about gay marriage, between those in favor of it and those against. As with many issues, it is an important issue to discuss. As I perused social media last week, there were many statements that were uplifting and positive.

However, there were many comments that turned the debate into an ugly, negative, insulting, hateful discourse. From people on both sides of this issue. Reading those comments was disturbing to me. I had a visceral reaction. It was as if I was listening to an argument that got more heated and vicious with every word. I eventually logged out of social media and went on to other things. I could not read another word.

Regardless of the issue up for debate, we have the right to express our thoughts, beliefs, opinions. If you do not share my opinion or belief, that is fine. We can agree to disagree. I will respect your opinion, and I expect that you will respect mine. That is the key to the expression of such passionate issues- respect. To express your opinion is one thing. To be negative or insulting when someone disagrees with you, or challenges your opinion, is another.

I don't have the right to be disrespectful, ugly, hateful in my comments to another human being for any reason. Neither does anyone else.

Respect is given where respect is given.

The Bigger Picture

The Moon   April 6, 2013

I have been fortunate in my new life as a poet. I have met many artists from many different types of art. The other day I met a man, a poet. He is as enthralled with the moon as I am.

As long as humans have existed, we have had a fascination with the moon. The moon has had a profound effect on humankind in many areas, including calendars, days of the week, religion, art, literature, music, science, mythology. In urban lore, it can make a person turn into a werewolf. The moon can make a person go insane-hence the term "lunatic." Our name for the first day of the week is taken from the moon.

Prehistoric humans made carvings about the moon. Stonehenge and other lunar temples were created 5,000 years before Christ. People tracked the phases of the moon for information about growing and harvesting crops. The waves in the ocean are under the spell of the moon.

There is something that draws us to the moon. It is an inexplicable phenomenon. The moon has been the subject of many poems, operas, works of art, religions. There is an intangible link between us and the moon. It has existed since the world was created.

My link to the moon began three years ago. I met and fell in love with a man who loves the moon. I am no longer in love with this man. But my love for the moon continues unabated. I even call myself "The Poet of the Moon."

Many see different things when gazing at the moon. Some see the rabbit in the moon. Some see the man in the moon. Some see the moon as a god. Others as a goddess. I've heard that, when a mime looks at the moon, they see a face like theirs, also in white.

When you look at the moon, what happens to you? What do you think of? What do you see? For me, I see a source of inspiration. I see comfort. I see loved ones in heaven. I see compassion. I see a companion. I see a generous, faithful muse that inspires me in my writing.

We are all under the spell of the moon. We are all under its enchantment. It is our constant friend and guardian.

Our protector. Our inspiration. Our constant companion in the universe.

The moon is always there for us. We are never alone.

> *"Her antiquity in preceding and surviving succeeding tellurian generations: her nocturnal predominance: her satellitic dependence: her luminary reflection: her constancy under all her phases, rising and setting by her appointed times, waxing and waning: the forced invariability of her aspect: her indeterminate response to inaffirmative interrogation: her potency over effluent and refluent waters: her power to enamour, to mortify, to invest with beauty, to render insane, to incite to and aid delinquency: the tranquil inscrutability of her visage: the terribility of her isolated dominant resplendent propinquity:*
> *her omens of tempest and of calm:*
> *the stimulation of her light, her motion and her presence: the admonition of her craters, her arid seas, her silence: her splendour, when visible: her attraction, when invisible."*
> *— James Joyce, "Ulysses"*

The Bigger Picture

Creating a Destiny April 10, 2013

Life is an amazing thing. It moves by so quickly. With that in mind, I thought I would give you an update on things since I wrote "My Story."

Things have been going well. I began this blog last December. My reason for changing blogs was ease of use for you, the reader.

This blog has over 60 languages. You can select the language you want, and have my poetry translated into your language. To date this blog has had over 5,100 visitors.

As I have grown as a poet and an artist, I began to think about publishing my work. I have done much research on the subject. I have decided that the best way to publish my poetry is to do it myself.

I have been working on compiling my poetry for months, getting it ready for print. The books are now in the editorial stage.

There are 4 books in all that I want to publish: two in English, two in Spanish, in print and electronic format.

I have also been building a website for my new publishing company. There are a few things missing; however, those are details that will come with time.

Yesterday I met with a lawyer to discuss how to create my own publishing company. He gave me a list of things to do. **"First you need to do this, and then you need to that."**

The meeting with the lawyer was free through my local library.

It saved me hundreds of dollars. That meeting was just one of the steps I am taking on this journey.

Things are now moving forward at an amazing speed.

My company should be ready in about a months' time, and the books should be ready to print then as well.

I hope to have the books available for purchase this fall, or around Christmas time.

Beginning this new venture in my life, this new adventure, I feel like I am on a thousand mile journey.

My journey has begun, and I am only a quarter of the way.

There will be many steps on this journey, many obstacles to overcome, many dragons to slay.

I feel like I'm not just creating a business. I'm not just creating a publishing house.

I'm not just becoming an entrepreneur and publisher. I'm not just publishing books of my poetry.

I'm creating a destiny.

The Bigger Picture

The Writer's Eye   April 24, 2013

It seems that writers look at the world differently than others do, with a detailed eye. Each writer has their own unique view of the world, their own unique eye that helps them see, perceive, detect.

Each eye is as unique and varied as the writers themselves. Some writer's eyes are like kaleidoscopes, some are like magnifying glasses, mirrors, even indigo colored glasses.

Once the writer discovers their eye, it then becomes a tool for examining themselves and the world around them. It is a wonderful tool of self-expression, self-exploration, and knowledge of the self.

The writer is then blessed with enhanced clarity, vision, wisdom and insight into themselves, their friends, loved ones, patterns, behaviors, pathologies, even the world itself.

The writer's eye does help us writers understand the world around us, and our place in it. We do see the world differently. I see myself differently. It has been a profound resource for me.

Before I found my eye, it was like I was looking at the world through a peephole in a door. The door has opened, and I am met with a massive view of the world. My eyes have adjusted to the once blinding light.

I can now use the eye I have been given, to see the world, and within. The writer's eye is an immense gift. I don't know why or how I got it. But I'm sure glad I have it.

The Bigger Picture

Blissfully Foolish May 1, 2013

(A letter to the moon)

Hello Luna, my dear friend. I saw you at my window the other night. That was so sweet of you to come and give me comfort. Somehow you always know when I need you. You are always there for me. Did you hear my news? I formed my new company! I named it after you. It seems only right, given our special bond.

There certainly is a strong bond between us. How did that happen? Well, I know how it happened-I fell in love with a man who loved you. I came to know you through him and grew to love you too. But it is not just with me; you have a strong bond with many. I have heard tell of people staring at you for hours, even to the point of lunacy. Maybe they are enraptured by your beauty. But, that cannot be all of it. You are like us; your true beauty lies within. I have heard people say that you are a mirror, reflecting our own inner beauty back to us. I have also heard that when people look at you, they see the thing or person they most love. (I have to confess, hearing that phrase made me think of a certain mirror in those famous wizard books.) I guess to some that could be true.

But, when I see you, I see a guardian. A muse. A companion. A friend. I recently heard that song about you. Have you heard it yet? You probably have-it is a couple of years old by now. I couldn't believe one of the lines in the song; it said that people are fools if they talk to you! Maybe I am a fool. Maybe writing to you like this, in a way talking to you, is foolish. If that is the case, so be it. I pray I live the rest of my days being unabashedly and blissfully foolish.

Take care of yourself my Luna, my moon. Talk to you soon, my eternal best friend.

The Bigger Picture

Citizen of the World   May 7, 2013

Have you ever wondered how you got where you are? Have you ever wondered how your people arrived where you are now? Have you ever wondered about your ancestry? Your heritage? Your lineage?

Shortly after I was born I was adopted. My parents are of Scottish/Irish/English ancestry. When they adopted me, I adopted their ancestry.

Many adopted children grow up to be adults that want to find their birth parents. I don't blame someone for wanting to do that, to find the parents that gave birth to them. But it is not for me.

I have seen many shows on television dealing with ancestry, finding links throughout the world through DNA, (Deoxyribonucleic acid), the building blocks of life. Since seeing these shows, I have wanted to do this myself.

This year for my birthday one of my sisters gave me a voucher for a DNA kit. The company in question divides the world into 5 regions (instead of the 7 continents.) The final results would show me what countries had matches for my DNA, based on those 5 regions.

I entered the information for the voucher online; a few weeks later I received my kit. I followed the instructions, swabbed the inside of my cheek, sealed the samples in an envelope, and sent them back to the company. A few weeks later I now have my results.

Going in, I thought Ireland would be the top of the list for a DNA match. I was told that the name of my birth parents is Irish.

The Bigger Picture

I love Irish music; it speaks to my soul like no other. I would have bet money that the number one country match would have been Ireland. That's not what I found out.

I received an e-mail today that my results were ready. I went to a website, logged in, and saw my results. I saw that there was a list of top country matches in each region, and how my DNA matched (or did not match) other countries in the same region.

I mainly concentrated on the top 5 countries, the countries with the strongest match.

Here then are my results. My DNA was found in the following countries:

Greece-Afghanistan-Honduras-Rwanda-Australia

Seeing these results makes me think back to the time of Pangea, the immense continent that once contained all 7 continents. With that image in mind, these results make sense. We were once all connected. We are all connected still.

I don't know which of the 5 countries or regions has the stronger link. I don't know which country is my country of origin. It could be one of those 5, or another country all together.

(If I want to do one, I can do an ancestry test, also using DNA, to find my actual country of origin. But, the test is $100; I probably won't be doing that.)

I don't know where my ancestors came from, or how they came to the U.S. It is understood, being an American, that other than the Native American Indian tribes, everyone else came to this country somehow.

The Bigger Picture

As my President said, the U.S. is:
    "...a nation of immigrants."-Barack Obama

Our ancestors came here. Somehow. It's the same for you. Some way, somehow, we all got where we are now.

I knew that I was American, and something else too. But I did not know what.

Now I know-I am:
           American
           Scottish
           Irish
           English
           Grecian
           Afghani
           Honduran
           Rwandan
           and
           Australian!

We were once all connected. We are all connected still.

It is the same for all of us. I am just like you.

I am a citizen of the world.

Confidence

May 11, 2013

As I have written before, I have two kittens, "Kit" and "Caboodle." The two kittens are almost a year old. It is fun to watch them play together, sometimes wrestling, sometimes galloping through the house as if they were wild stallions.
I love to see them interact together, teach each other things, cuddle with each other.

Yesterday, I bought the kittens some new toys. One of the toys I bought is a plastic wand with a long strip of fabric on the end of it. To play with it, the human waves the wand and the piece of fabric moves on the floor (or through the air.) The cat then follows the piece of fabric and plays with it, as if it is a snake or similar animal. It brings out their hunting instincts, and is a natural form of play.

I brought the toy out for the kittens to play with. To my shock, they were terrified; they ran and hid under the bed. It did not take me long to figure out why they were afraid-they had never seen a toy like that before.

I spoke to them in a calming tone, telling them that everything was alright, and that they would love this new toy. I walked past my bed, carrying the wand, slowly dragging the piece of fabric on the floor. Instinct got the better of "Kit" and she bounded right out from under the bed. Within 5 minutes I had her hooked.

As the time passed "Kit's" confidence grew, and she became more self-assured with the toy. A few minutes later, "Caboodle" came out from hiding. She watched "Kit" playing with it, and learned how to do it. Within 5 minutes both "Kit" and "Caboodle" were playing with the toy. Their moments of absolute terror ended in an evening of frolic and delight with their new toy.

The Bigger Picture

That experience with the kittens last night reminded me of when I began to write. True, I never ran from a room in terror and hid under a bed at the thought of having to write something. But I was very insecure about writing, at first. It was something I had never really done before.

I was encouraged to begin writing three years ago, by a few friends, as a means of self-expression, to convey my thoughts and emotions. I remember sharing my writings with these new friends and being completely insecure. I would ask things like:

> "Did you like it? Did you understand it?
> Do you understand why I said that?
> What did you think about it?"

I was like the terrified kitten with the new toy. I didn't know if I was writing correctly, conveying what I really wanted to say, or even writing in a way that anyone besides me would understand. My friends filled the mentor role, as I did with the kittens. They assured me they liked what I wrote and encouraged me to continue.

I used to ask my friends what they thought about something I'd written. I was very insecure. I did not think I had any talent as a writer at all. My friends reassured me and told me that my writing was very good, and that I should continue. Honestly, I thought they were placating me. As I wrote more and shared my poems with friends my confidence grew.

One day, I asked a friend what he would think about my creating a blog of my writing. He greatly encouraged me to do so. I told him I could never do that; share my deepest thoughts and feelings with the world. That's when Esperanza Habla was born.

Writing under the pen name Esperanza Habla gives me the confidence I needed to express what I want to say. I have a new found confidence in myself. I am not the person I was three years ago. I also have confidence in my writing.

I write a poem and post it; I don't ask anyone's opinion about it. However, sometimes I will get comments from my blog readers. They tell me:
> **"You are so good at writing." "Keep writing."**
> **"I read your poem; it really helped me."**
> **"Reading your poem, I felt what you felt."**
> **"Your poetry is so universal-everyone can relate."**
> **"I love what you wrote. Keep writing."**

Although I don't solicit these comments, they are very encouraging to me. I love hearing that I have helped someone. That is a precious feeling to me.

I have truly grown in confidence over the last three years. I became a writer. I became Esperanza Habla. I have grown into a poet with one blog, and now a second. I have grown into a publisher, forming my own publishing company to publish my written works. None of this would have ever happened, or maybe happened in this way, without those initial friends' words of encouragement.

I recently heard a quote that says:
> ***"The master opens the door,***
> ***but only you can enter."***

I want to thank my friends for being the masters that opened the door for me, encouraging me to write, believing in me. I want to thank myself, and Esperanza Habla, for having the confidence to walk through.

About the Author

Esperanza Habla is the pen name of the Indigo Poet of the Moon. She began her writing career in 2010. She has had two blogs to date, "Words of Hope" and "Letters to the Moon", which has garnered a readership in more than 75 countries worldwide.

In 2013 she formed her own publishing company, La Luna Press, L.L.C. Esperanza's first book of poetry, "I am Hope", was published in April of 2015.

Esperanza holds a degree in Music History and Literature from Marian University. Esperanza has been featured in the Poetry Daily and has received a nomination for an Indiana Authors Award in both 2015 and 2016.

This is her second book published in English.

www.lalunapress.com
www.esperanzahabla.com

Other publications from La Luna Press:

I am Hope

The first poetic collection by Esperanza Habla

Soy Esperanza

El primer colección poética por Esperanza Habla

www.lalunapress.com

www.ingramcontent.com/pod-product-compliance
Lightning Source LLC
Chambersburg PA
CBHW042303150426
43196CB00005B/63